Everything's a Verb

Everything's a
VERB

POEMS
Debra Marquart

Minnesota Voices Project Number 70

New Rivers Press 1995

New Rivers Press is a non-profit literary press dedicated to publishing the very best emerging writers in our region, nation, and world.

The publication of *Everything's a Verb* has been made possible by generous grants from the Dayton Hudson Foundation on behalf of Dayton's and Target Stores, the Jerome Foundation, the Metropolitan Regional Arts Council (from an appropriation by the Minnesota Legislature), the North Dakota Council on the Arts, the South Dakota Arts Council, and the James R. Thorpe Foundation.

Additional support has been provided by the Bush Foundation, the General Mills Foundation, Liberty State Bank, the McKnight Foundation, the Minnesota State Arts Board (through an appropriation by the Minnesota Legislature), the Star Tribune/Cowles Media Company, the Tennant Company Foundation, and the contributing members of New Rivers Press. New Rivers Press is a member agency of United Arts.

New Rivers Press books are distributed by The Talman Company, 131 Spring Street, Suite 201 E-N, New York, NY 10012 (1-800-537-8894).

Everything's a Verb has been manufactured in the United States of America for New Rivers Press, 420 N. 5th Street/Suite 910, Minneapolis, MN 55401. First Edition.

To Peter
and
for Lydia

Acknowledgments

Grateful acknowledgments to the editors of the following magazines in which some of these poems first appeared, sometimes in earlier versions:

Charlotte Poetry Review, Circumference, Cumberland Poetry Review, Half Tones to Jubilee, Loonfeather, Poet Lore, Southern Poetry Review, and *Zone 3*.

"Finding the Words," "Somewhere in a House Where You are Not," and "Speaking the Language" appeared in *Clearing Space Anthology* (Wordshop, Inc., 1993).

"History of a Portrait," "I am Upstairs, Trying to Be Quiet," and "The Long Root" appeared in a chapbook, *A Circle of Four* (Dacotah Territory Press, 1989).

Line from "homage to my hips" by Lucille Clifton is reprinted from *two-headed woman* by permission of Curtis Brown, Ltd. © 1980 by University of Massachusetts Press.

Line from John Berger's essay "Her Secrets" originally appeared in *Three Penny Review,* © 1986 by John Berger.

The line from Thomas McGrath's *Letter to an Imaginary Friend* is used with permission from Thomas McGrath's estate.

The author wishes to thank Iowa State University for a Pearl Hogrefe Fellowship that enabled this work to be completed, and a special thanks to Bill Truesdale who labored so patiently over this book.

Contents

The Long Root

This Room Full of Nothing

Truly, we writers are the secretaries of death.

—John Berger

Places
Only the
Body
Knows

Speaking the Language

Again the language fails me
trying to describe her.
Words fragment on my tongue.
Vowels roll into tomatoes
ripening on her windowsill.
Consonants clatter and stack
neatly in her cupboard.

She taught me to speak
this language. She said,
I am very exciting, meaning
she was looking forward
to something. She said, *bodado*,
that small white vegetable
she peeled each day, her hand
riding high on the blade
of a paring knife, her fingers
permanently bent to the shape
of a medium-sized potato.

She said, *uppsie daisy,*
pulling me to her large
round bosom long after
I was too heavy to lift.
She said, That was good, *not?*
meaning, Don't you think so?

How do I decipher
this language she left me.
These recipes for knephla
and strudel that never include
flour—flour being the ingredient

too obvious for her to mention.
These recipes that do not tell
how many minutes to bake
or at what temperature.

Lost to me, all of it,
like the magnet earrings
she promised
out of her jewelry box
that were baubles in front,
and magnets in back,
that did not pierce
or clip, that held
the earring to the lobe
by some rare, invisible power.

When the Names Still Fit the Faces

On a shelf in the back of the big closet
after her death we found stacks and stacks

of photo albums full of her subjects. How many
did she fool with her stammering *just-a-second,*

her fiddling, *this darn thing,* her eye stalling
for the perfect cinematic moment, that infinity

of seconds when genuine smiles stretch thin
and elastic, when loose arms thrown casually

over shoulders grow heavy. The early photos
feature plain women in fancy dresses, and new cars

parked by old houses. The later photos are thick
with nyloned thighs, Christmas trees dripping

with ornaments, uncles long dead and children
long grown old. Surely, this is the trail

she would have us follow, back to the people
we would never know, the selves we would never

recall, back to the time when the names
still fit the faces. In the end fearing loss

of memory she took to labeling every photo,
putting the name, finally, to the image,

sprawling *Ed* across Ed's blank forehead,
tracing *Reinhold* on a high, thin, cheekbone,

spiraling *Emma* up Emma's bleach-blonde
beehive. She, the hand behind the shutter

is seldom pictured. Only in rare moments
when someone has seized the camera

and forced her into the frame
does she appear—grinning, big-boned,

and out of context—with a large *Me*
emblazoned across her bosom.

Behave

On TV when the cops crash
through your door they scream,
Stop, or I'll shoot, but I recall
a newly-minted deputy
storming our kegger years ago.
Fingers itchy for the stiff leather
of his holster, he made for
the bonfire yelling, Shoot,
or I'll stop. Such things

stay with you, like the way
my ex used to say, Now you
just behave, when he thought
my neck had slipped too far
out of the loop of his noose.
I'd curl my legs under me,
and purr, Oh sure, honey,
I'm *being-have*, pronouncing it
with a slight southern accent,
a word like a silk sheet
slipping, perfectly,
off my tongue. But you know

how it is with cats, all sweetness
curled on the couch
when you're home,
but shredding their nails
on the chiffon as your car
backs down the driveway.
Don't kid yourself,
they're looming large
over the gerbil and pissing
wild arcs into the flowerpot,
even as your garage door
yawns to its slow mechanical

close. Lately I've been thinking
about the word, *behave*,
how it's made entirely of verbs,
but it's all about getting nowhere.
Being-have means, *being had*,
means, *having been*, means,
being a has-been. It reminds me

of the way I could never breathe,
when I was a kid, that long, slow
hyperventilating experience
of childhood. I'd go white and claw
my neck. My sisters would turn
and groan, Dad, she's doing it

again. And Dad would get
his red face right next to mine,
hunker down as if to adjust
the TV, and scream, Now you
just relax. Sure, the air of fear

rushed greedily into my lungs.
But even though they all believed
it had worked, I always knew
it hadn't.

Wormwood

My father tells the story
he has told every day of his life,
of the woman brought from the south

where they still practiced the old ways,
when Doc Simon said there was no hope
because fluid was in both of his young lungs,

how the uncles fetched her by carriage
on the shortest day of winter,
how she dug deep under tall banks

for wormwood, a grayish-greenish
stinky weed that no one, not even
the herefords would eat, how she

boiled milk and dropped the leaves
in, how she made a bitter soup
for him to drink. Here my father

sits back and breathes deep
wormwood's tale—little leaf,
tiny slip, smuggled through Customs

years ago inside some washerwoman's
sleeve. He has reached the border
of what he knows. What lies beyond

is unknown country, a tangled
wilderness of sheets, soaked
with sweat, cold rags pressed

to a burning forehead, prayers,
whispering over him in the night.
Beyond this point lives gossip,

hearsay, the places only the body
knows. Here my father's hands
grow wings, as if forming the story

from air, the old blue veins tracing
the slow curve of memory. *They say
she named the fever "little fire"*

*and warned it to find a better place
to burn.* When lost, he invents details—
the dozen eggs she took in payment

for her work—but he always keeps
the ending the same. How Doc Simon
asked about him, some weeks later

not seeing a notice of death
in the news. How Grandpa said,
Wormwood. How Doc Simon said,

That could have killed him.

And Who Do You Belong To?

Even in my ghost costume
I'm recognizable,
with my three older sisters
the nun, the witch and
the pirate, who are only in it
for the candy, and my brother,
who believes he is Napoleon.

It's not the question,
*And what are you supposed
to be?* that bothers me.
Under my clean, white sheet,
it's apparent, I'm a ghost.
It's the other question,
And who do you belong to?
that sets our feet shuffling.
Our answer, like a chicken bone,
we hold in our throats
considering treachery,
until finally, the nun
spits it out, our father's
name. And that is when

the wife calls the husband
off the couch, the dog
comes too, and even the parrot
takes note, it's Felix's kids
at their front door mercy.
We are the children
of the year-round trickster.
Felix, who pokes every chest
for the invisible stain. Felix of
I got your nose, I got your nose

fame. And tonight we go
door-to-door, forced to
wait out the good laugh.

And I begin to cry,
I'm so tired of people laughing,
and I cry straight through to
the St. Philip's party
when the Sisters ask,
how many jelly beans
in this jar? I get weepy then

because I only know up to ten,
so my sister, the pirate,
guesses for me, writing down
one number less
than her own guess,
and I end up winning
the whole goddamn jar.

The Permanent

The wind that blew me from the porch
that afternoon came out of the dusty nowhere

that is the high plains. My mother, inside,
winding Grandma's fine feathers into pink,

permanent rollers, did not see the rock
that knocked a hole in my skull,

could not stop to watch the blood
rush from the wound, only heard the wail

wind up, the siren song that blew long after
the gush had stopped, long after the rush

of water and my sisters' shampooing hands
had washed it all away. Mother applied

the permanent solution, guaranteeing
grandma's curls were now a matter of record.

The skunky smell of permanent drifted
from the kitchen, the rotten egg odor permeated

all the rooms. Grandma took me to her lap,
that great lost continent of thigh. Let me see,

she said, tilting my cracked egg head
to the side. Oy, yoy, yoy, she clicked

her tongue with regret. *Oy, yoy, yoy.*
That's going to be permanent.

Motorcade

From here it becomes necessary
to ship all bodies east.

—Thomas McGrath

I was seven when it happened
in the second grade, but old enough
to know it was serious
when Sister Jacinta, bleary-eyed
and wrinkled, announced
that our Catholic President
had been shot. We rose,
hands over our hearts to say
the Pledge-Allegiance, then hands
together to pray the Our-Father
although, I believe, all along,
we understood we were praying
for the soul and not the man.

What I remember most is Ronnie Bissell
sneezing through everything.
A tin of pepper on his desk,
for what I don't recall
perhaps show-and-tell,
but some dark itching powder
had gotten into his nose.
And somehow I've always known
that he enjoyed it,
the body betraying itself
at that very solemn moment.
He was the flamboyant one,
class clown, moved away
after graduation, like all of us.
I never heard from him again
until last year when I saw
his obituary in the paper:
still single, his address
listed as San Francisco. Bodies

are flowing back to us from places
less parochial. How immune
we believed ourselves to be
so far from the swirling locus
of events. There are moments
like these in history
that hold themselves up
like great roaring surfaces,
too large to reveal anything,
but that one single frame
from the movie
of our own lives. That night,

we watched it on the news:
the motorcade running the gauntlet.
President Kennedy alive and smiling
then dead, alive and smiling,
then dead. Jackie in her pillbox hat
and short waist-coat, crawling
onto the trunk of the convertible,
almost reaching the arms
of the secret service man, almost
going backward for one long moment,
while all else rushed forward,
then thinking better
and returning to the back seat,
to her already dead husband,
the motorcade picking up speed
and accelerating madly
out of view of the camera.

I am Upstairs, Trying to Be Quiet

when i think of her, i think of silence,
my mouth growing tight across my face
after she has told me not to sing
in the house, not to move around so much,
told me she could fix dinner twice
in the time it would take to show me once,
what i would only forget
and have to be shown again anyway,
and how i would only make a mess
that she would have to clean up later.
i hear a cupboard door slam.
she is in the kitchen with father,
talking about lazy kids.
i am upstairs, trying to be quiet.
even though i'm safe in my room
with the door shut, i know she
can still hear me breathing.
often now when i dream,
i dream of that place. things
follow me there i cannot stop—
street gangs, rock bands, nazis.
it's different every time. i hear them
downstairs, trashing the furniture,
raiding the refrigerator and leaving
their scraps on the kitchen table.
they are playing the stereo loud
and having their women in her bedroom.
i want to stop them, but there's nothing
i can do. the sounds come to me
like hard fists in my sleep. i am upstairs,
trying to be quiet. downstairs,
they are tearing her limb from limb.

Birthmark

It has been seventy-two hours
since he last slept. I have been

counting. He has rummaged
through the drawers, muttering

to himself. He has threatened the lives
of all the major appliances.

It has been seventy-two hours
and now he is asleep. The room

is like a vault when I go upstairs
to check. The air is stale.

The curtains drawn.
In this big bed, he is nothing more

than a spill of black hair, the tension
of his jaw let loose, the beacon

in his forehead extinguished.
I check his heart first

then his covers. He is overheated.
All over his skin is damp

and rosy. I touch the white
streak in his hair, a birthmark

from the tongs where the doctors
tried to extract him

from his mother. Born with a black
eye on Friday the thirteenth,

he came out fighting, he said,
because he didn't want to come out

at all. The garbage man
is outside with his clanking cans

and backup bell. I cover
his ears and he wraps himself

around me. I cover his ears
and he wraps himself around

the wideness of my hips.

Between Wives

I was trying to teach him a lesson
      that day she stepped in
with her wide skirts, her sing-song
      assurances. I was trying to kill

the thing in him that was killing me.
      At the Village Inn, she and I
are having one of those civil discussions
      women have after everything's over.

He's at home, fuming through
      half-packed rooms as we drain cup
after cup over the subject of him. Listen,
      I say, quoting Heinemann, a curious thing

has happened to our generation of men.
      There were the guys that went to Vietnam,
and the guys that, for whatever reason,
      did not go. I tell her this because

she's too young to know. Your eyes,
      she says, are the most amazing green.
She is like this: all lies and diversions.
      My eyes are the harsh lens he has seen

himself through for seven years. Love,
      I say, pouring my tenth cup, love is like
a ferris wheel. Sometimes the damn thing
      creaks to a halt and, if you're on bottom

you have the option of getting off. Her eyes
      are clear blue, tears welling up
as she says, let me know if you want back on,
      because I will get out of the way

for you. If I wanted you out of the way,
   I say, lifting a finger, I would move you.
But it's all smoke I'm blowing.
   I am the second wife; soon she will be

the third, and I will be the nightmare
   he had between wives. The waiter
appears, all concern. He checks
   the thermos and slides the bill

perfectly between us. What if
   I told you, she says, reaching across
the table, that your precious wheel
   has started up without you. Sister,

I think, oh sister,
   how I want to kiss you full
on those lips he loves and let loose
   this thing that rattles

in my chest. *Remember to keep*
   the angle of your vision wide
when he comes swinging, I want to say,
   but I swallow these words

like a bad meal and retreat to the wisdom
   of experts. According to Heinemann,
I offer, like one who has read
   an informative news report on the subject,

a split has erupted in our generation
   of men. A dialogue has yet to occur
between them. Try to remember that, I say,
   that is the killing thing about him.

He Will Make Some Woman

A trail of wringing hands
leading back to mother
follows him. He will make

some woman forget
biological timeclocks,
cling to spare moments

before motocross,
parachutes, and third worlds
claim him. Willingly,

he will go, gearing up
and slapping backs
all the way. He'll stand

in open ground during air raids,
turn over poker tables
in hot, smoky rooms.

Like Burt Lancaster
in *From Here to Eternity*,
he'll jump into street brawls,

kicking the knife
out of Fatso's hand,
his shirt tail

will stay trimly tucked,
one button will open
at the collar. He will find

some woman who handles
a kerchief well, a woman
who looks good in gloves.

He will give her
a solid reason
to wear black.

Missing Wife

The poster at the truck stop
says she suffers bouts
of amnesia, wanders off,
forgets she is his wife.
The husband is asking around.
Has anyone seen her?
There's a reward, in heavy
black letters, a phone number
and photos of Saturday night
drinking beer on the couch,
and of a wedding, the man
looking sharp in his tuxedo,
the woman in her veil
looking like a tumbleweed
of lace. They are smiling,
cutting the cake. His hand
over hers on the glistening
white knife. This woman

could be anyone. Out there,
walking the street, warming
her face in the afternoon sun,
she is trying new foods
and buying exotic clothes
without the prior knowledge
of her husband. She has not
forgotten how, in the early days
he woke her, doing the soft shoe,
singing, *Good morning, baby,*
how did you sleep?
Nor has she forgotten
the black line of his moustache
hurrying over her, some nights,
as if she were a dark room
he could never find
the switch for. How it came

to his hands around
her throat she does not know.
But she will never forget
her own voice, hoarse,
and no longer her own,
begging him to do it,
do it, to *just fucking*
do it. It was not forgetting

that took this woman.
It was, rather, a rare case
of remembering—remembering
how every day he drew a line
for her, and how she secretly
kept track, by notching the floorboard
where the last line had been.
And after a time she saw
he was cheating her, by fractions
until all that was left
was that immaculate white line
and the blank wall,
against which she posed
for all the pictures
he took of her.

Finding the Words

When I walk it,
the path to the lost words
will be strewn with socks,
gloves, earrings, all the twins
of things I've lost
on this long journey out.
I'll gather them up like toys
in my skirt, following the thin trail,
this hedge I have kept against
famine, fatigue and loss
of direction. I'll search

for signposts, rings of keys,
all eighteen pairs of sunglasses
ever lost to me. All the fifty-second cards
to the decks I never played, will slip
from my sleeves. Every dead letter
will be returned to me. Along the road,

I'll have a chance to see
my old three dogs named Tippy,
Susie, my one-eyed cat,
all the grandparents,
all the greats and even
my virginity will flush out
from somewhere, pull the last
mauve ribbon from my hair,
as I pass, reeling, now,
in a chariot drawn
by furious stallions,
their crazy manes blazing
a path through the deepest part
of the woods. The forest,
bending to greet us,

leads us to the clearing
where burns the fire that burns
from the center of the earth.

It is here I will dance
my warrior dance, pounding
my feet into the dirt.
I will sit down and sing
this plain song,
long and low and sweet.
Syllables flying
from my tongue
like sparks
from a chip of flint.

A
Regular
Dervish

True Tribe

don't give me that blood-follows-blood
crap, i want a new tribe. i came through
my mother's water and my father's fire
to get here. my skin may be the color
of newly fallen snow, but i dye my hair
jet black because in art I learned
that a paintbrush dipped many times
in water makes this color. i am not
the unmarked canvas, i am dark water,
and today i'm a black-haired white girl
walking down the street who sees herself
only in the store window's reflection.
i get happy, for instance, when a sioux man
stops me on the sidewalk for a quarter and asks,
what's your tribe. wanting new ancestors,
i say, i'm the daughter of meat-eaters,
who is no longer hungry. this is a lie
(note the leather jacket, shoes, belt).
i learned such duplicity from my grandmother,
of german blood, during world war ii,
who shamed us, shamed us, who
shamed us into america. truthfully,
i'm the daughter of men who scaled
continents to escape learning how
to stand in formation and shoot. farmers
who inhabited land, flat and rolling,
good for planting crops, also good
for waves of advancing troops. hey,
(this is our family boast)
some of the best generals in history
have left our tender roots
trampled in fields.
searching for my true tribe,
i trace the almond shapes

of my eyes, wanting, with the heat
of sex, a hun invader,
knocking down the door
to be my distant grandfather.
not for the victimhood of it, no,
but just to say that something old
and bloody survives in me.
whatever comes to this life,
comes to it through violence.
we live in a country
that dispatches B-2 bombers
if our winter shipment
of kiwi fruit is late.
try to wash the mess
of that, the mess of that,
try to wash
that mess
from your hands.

Getting Ready

i'm the thousand-change girl,
getting ready for school,
standing in my bedroom,
ripping pants and shirts
from my body, trying dresses
and skirts. my father,

at the bottom of the steps
is yelling, the bus
is coming, here comes
the bus. i'm wriggling
into jeans, zippers
grinding their teeth,
buttons refusing
their holes. my brother,

dressed-in-five-minutes,
stands in the hallway,
t-shirt and bookbag
saying, what's the big
problem. i'm kneeling
in front of the closet
foraging for that great-lost-
other-shoe. downstairs,
my father offers advice. slacks,
he's yelling, just put on
some slacks. i'm in the mirror
matching earrings,
nervous fingers
putting the back
to the front. downstairs

the bus is fuming in the yard,
farm kids with cowlicks
sitting in rows. everything's

in a pile on the floor.
after school, mother will scream,
get upstairs and hang up
that mess, but i don't care.
I'm the thousand-change girl,
trotting downstairs now
looking good, looking ready

for school. father, pulling back
from the steps with disgust,
giving me the once over,
saying, is *that*
what you're wearing.

Doing the Twist

Felix has four daughters
just like the Lennon sisters
on the Lawrence Welk television
show. Felix has four daughters,
two altos and two sopranos,
but wouldn't you know,
Felix can't get those girls
to stand together in a straight row,
much less wear the same clothes.
Felix says, I've got four daughters
for all the good it's doing me.
One night, watching the TV, Felix calls
into the kitchen, says, look here girls,
come and see this fellow dancing.
Come and see this crazy
Chubby Checkers. The girls
crowd the doorway, watching
Chubby grind out cigarettes
on the Ed Sullivan show.
One by one, they drop
their shoes. One by one,
they drop their dishtowels,
and in their stocking feet,
they try it, careful at first
on the hardwood floor, doing
the twist. What is going on?
Gladys calls from the kitchen,
doing the dishes by herself.
They're busy, Felix yells,
they're doing the twist.
After this, they do it
for holidays and company
and whenever relatives come
from California. Felix goes

to Bismarck and buys
the record and damn
if those girls can't dance,
twisting in a diamond,
like all the points
on a compass.
The sopranos twisting high,
the altos twisting low,
and the youngest one, they say,
is a regular dervish.

Watching Joann Castle Play

Saturday nights, before Mom and Dad
went to polka, we'd watch Lawrence Welk.
We'd watch Bobby throw Cissy and catch her.
Joe Feeney sang *My Wild Irish Rose*.
Arthur Duncan tap danced across the stage.
Lawrence emceeing in that corny German brogue
my father did not hesitate to remind us
he laughed all the way to the bank with.
Everybody singing, everybody swaying
in chiffon and sports coats, everybody smiling
those *that's-entertainment-the-show-
must-go-on-there's-no-business-like-
show-business* smiles. There was one woman
we waited for and that was Joann Castle.
Joann Castle with her mile-high, honey-blonde
beehive, and her big, big back that never quite fit
into her big backless gowns. Joann Castle
with her hands on the keys, playing
the honky tonk. As we watched from behind
Lawrence counted her off *a one and a two*
and away she would go, her bare arms
flapping her big bottom bouncing,
she'd be jamming the keys, rapping,
like tongues they were flapping.
When she turned to face the camera,
her pearly whites, still tinkling those ivories.
Even the fogeys in the back row felt inclined
to say, Joann Castle, man. She's been to Chicago.
She's been to New York. Shit man, I'll bet
she's even been to New Orleans.

The Woman on the Dance

these hips are mighty hips
these hips are magic hips
— Lucille Clifton

The woman
the woman
the woman on the dance
                         floor's hips
do not sway or dip or grind.
     They only *swish bump swish bump*
          swish through the songs
     strung together like the beads
on the chain around
her neck.

                    The woman on the dance
          floor's hips do not have
     a country, did not vote
for president,
     are scarcely connected
to the arms that rise
     to straighten a hair,
          to the eyes that turn
to study the drummer
     under hot flashing
          lights.

The woman
on the dance floor's hips
     are neutrons
          in an atom,
needing nothing to sustain them,
     nothing to sustain
          them, nothing.

The Attempt

i.

on ludes in the house with the big porch
on second street she tried to o.d. we,
driving by in our van happened to stop.
good thing. we sat, watched her breathe
her goodbyes into the phone. so as not to make
her heart race, we waited for the receiver
to drop. it did. we hauled her *one two*
into the van and drove to the hospital
two blocks away from the house with
the big porch on second street.

ii.

her mother that fluorescent light night,
wringing questions from her kerchief
into the purple seats, turned her knees
to mine, dumb, about the fists full
of ludes, the bags in her drawers,
the man she was doing this all for.

iii.

the next morning, hungry, in her hospital bed,
she asked me how she, last night, looked.
i said i didn't recall, only the medics
running with her, the doors flying open
ahead of us. i did not say only
all these years i cannot forget,
her blouse pulled up over her face,
her unsnapped bra, white
and flapping in the wind.

Bronze These Shoes

                    Peter says
I should bronze these platform shoes
that I found in a box marked *keepers*
in my parents' basement. Tan suede
with stars appliqued all around, heels
like paperweights, these shoes

were on my feet the day I went to
my Great Uncle Fred's funeral
and somehow it all comes back to me
when I see them—Fred ranging around
his big messy house in his wheelchair
for he had lost a leg to diabetes, and his wife,

Great Aunt Ida with her one gold tooth
and her cateye glasses, who liked to cook
but never liked to do dishes, who had
too many promiscuous daughters,
who stood on the front porch
and waved a hankie when you came

to visit. I wore these shoes
to Fred's funeral, and on that day
I wore a burnt orange minidress
that was all thigh and no hip,
and a heavy streak of eyeliner
and my hair was long and straight
and parted exactly down the middle.

And people took photos of Fred,
I recall, looking cool in his casket.
And all the ladies wept and sweated

in their big flowered dresses. And me,
tromping around, tugging at the hem
of my mini. And Ida, dabbing her eyes
with her hankie. All of us commenting
on how hard it was to believe that Fred

was actually gone. And I think about
those things we leave behind in boxes,
and about Ida who fell flat and died
in a K-Mart ten years later, rushing,
I've always liked to imagine
for some really good blue light special.

My Father Tells This Story about His Brother Frank and the Wick (Every Time I Ask Him For Money)

your grandpa marquart he was a tight sonofabitch, you know, every night he'd come to the bottom of the steps and yell up, frank, go to sleep, you're wasting my oil, because frank liked to read, he was always reading something. he wasn't much for farm work, but he liked school and reading and just wasting his time on books.

so grandpa thought he better put an end to all that laziness and sloth. frank was pretty much worthless when five o'clock chores rolled around. it was more work getting him out of bed than just doing the chores yourself.

so this went on for years, this, grandpa coming to the steps at night and yelling up, frank go to sleep, you're wasting my oil, and frank setting his book down, leaving it open to the last page he was reading and rolling the wick down into the lamp and dousing the flame.

so finally frank gets this town job and makes a little money, and the first thing he does is buys himself some oil right off, see, so he can read as late as he pleases. then when grandpa comes to the steps at night and yells up, frank, go to sleep, you're wasting my oil, frank gets out of bed and goes to the top of the steps and yells back down, this is my oil, I bought this oil with my own money, and I will burn this oil however I see fit.

but grandpa, he had a way, you know, of seeing how things broke down, how they divided up, because he yelled right back, without even thinking, he said, but what about the wick? that's what he said, what about the wick?

your grandfather, i'm telling you, now there was a tight man.

Shit & the Dream of It

All the arts derive from
this ur-act of making.

— W.H. Auden

I was knee-deep in my dad's polebarn,
below zero for two weeks, the milk cows
couldn't go outside. We just spread straw
over the freshest layer and hoped
for warmer weather. I was breaking open
those straw bales spreading them wide
with a pitchfork when I said, *hey*,
I'm breaking out of this hellhole.
But how far can you get? They say

little kids stand by the toi-toi
and wave bye-bye as the new thing
they made swirls away. It's a stage
they go through. I never went through
stages, I just hopped into whatever
had keys and hauled ass. Listen,

there's no escaping it. Last night
I dreamed I was naked on a commode
in the middle of a room full of high-up
mucky-mucks and they were all
drinking Chablis from some year
better than this one. The stool,
turns out, is an avant garde exhibit
of which I am a working part.
I'm in the center trying to produce
those gems they like, those necessary
nuggets. I cry for paper, a curtain
to wrap around me, but they say, no,
they're interested in process. Process,
I tell them, my ass. You know, my dad

tried to warn me that day I was peeling out
the driveway. Wherever you go, he said,
you'll find it. I don't mean to run on
like this, but he was right. One time,

at a party in the seventies some guy
took a crap on the livingroom carpet.
Tripping on acid, he mistook himself
for the family dog. He smelled that scent
and went for it. Now, you might want to say

that was the times, but listen,
I have plenty of relatives
planted in a hill just north
of my home town who will tell you
the rotten truth. Everything turns to it.
Just ask the worms. They'll give you
the straightest poop.

Everything's a Verb

boundaries
        or the lack thereof
                the counselor tries to tell me
        are the reason i am in this trouble
                i am in
the counselor wears
        a blunt cut   her blonde fingers delineate
                examples of boundary or lack thereof
        problems
(relationships with younger men
        relationships with older women
                this tendency i have of walking in to
        and out of
                marriages
        some of which were not
                my own) all clear cut examples
                        of boundary or lack thereof
                                problems
                        i try to explain
                how everything's a verb to me
        the world is an endless array of fibers
weaving and connecting
        unraveling as time passes   time
                                        itself a construct
                                loosely based upon our observations
                of the rate at which the threads go about
        this business of weaving and unraveling
the slower fibers becoming the things
        we name into nouns but they're all verbs
        if one is prepared to take the long view
                                        boundaries
                                the counselor reiterates
                        if i could establish clear-cut definitions
        between where i end

and the rest of the world
begins   i could put away
my dragon earrings   retire
my snake bracelets
cut loose once and for all
my junk yard dog
husband.

The Miracle Baby

She was born with a cunt and a brain.

That's the punchline to a joke told to me.
The question is *Have you heard about*

the miracle baby? and this guy has let me
in on it as if to say, I can tell you're one of those

unflappable broads who doesn't blanche
at the crude, who doesn't feel the whip

on her back, her hide has become so thick.
And I do not disappoint him, I smile

as if I have gotten it, and indeed
I have. Something is flexing in me,

forcing my rib cage wide, my throat
is tightening like a sphincter to contain

this blast that wants to belch out of me
hard like a fist and level everything.

this rage, I'm looking for the spell
to cure it. I'm trying to be the miracle baby,

but I must tell you these days
when I see these men led strictly

to me by their divining rods
something flashes and (I cannot stop

these thoughts) I see them naked
with their little wangers dangling,

and I want to snatch those tender
noodles, for this potion I'm concocting,

for this broth I am brewing,
for this sickness that burns

inside me. The recipe is old,
someone lost it long ago.

I'm making it up, making
it up. I'm forced

to make it up
as I go along.

Knitting

you with the knit-one-purl-two
you with the rosary on the nightstand
shoring up losses, worrying
the beads down to nothing
grandma, bean counter, the world
is unraveling since you left, the cat
got ahold of the skein, he's under
the couch, grandma, deeper
than i know how to go, my arms
are not enough, my arms
cannot reach, my baby
died on a friday, it was clear
the day you left, the cat
got ahold of the skein,
he's under the couch,
grandma, pulling, pulling
pulling those yarns, my arms
are not enough, my arms
cannot reach, my baby
died on a friday, my husband
thinks i'm
                grandma,
how many stitches in the row
after all that have dropped,
i cannot know, i cannot
know, i cannot know
how to pick them up

The
Long
Root

The Long Root

i.
She liked to tell jokes.
She told them good, in English,
pausing in the right places
just the way they had been told to her.
But when it came to punchlines,
she leaned toward Grandpa
and said it to him, in German.
The two of them would laugh and rock
in their seats. When I protested
she said, *there's no way to say,*
in English. Some small detour

of meaning, something lost
between the tongue and the brain.
There's no way to say this
in English. On her first trip

to the city she complimented me
on my lack of furniture
and fell upon my waterbed
with the zeal of a woman
who had never been. I left her there
to test it, returning to find her
grounded out on the sideboard—
her legs too short to reach
the floor, her bottom lodged
in the crack and too wide
to do anything about.

Help me out the bed, she said.
And we joined hands—me,

planting a foot and tugging;
she, rocking in the crevice,
until we laughed her loose.

                         Tonight
she is a horizontal ruin,
a mountain of secrets.
I have driven the deep funnel
of night, walked the endless
fluorescence of corridors
to witness this, her final trip
to the city. Her heartbeat
cuts a ragged path
on the glowing screen
above. She breathes
when the machine says so.
The nurses are familiar
with her body, rolling her over
saying, *Lydia, you bad girl,*
you have been throwing off
your covers again.

I am in the corner,
quiet as Lydia.
The nurses do not tell me
how sometimes the hearing
is the last to go.

ii.
I always wanted stories of the place
where she had come from.
I wanted stale bread
shared between many hands
and stony fields passed through
in the middle of the night.
I wanted superstitious women
dancing around campfires,
but when I asked she said,
you can't get there from here.
Some small detour of meaning,
something lost between the tongue
and the brain. Never long

on description, even less so now.
Lydia, bad girl, Black Sea German,
with a history of reinventing
the language. Secrets
were her craft, misinformation

her trade. When I got to the first grade
and found out somersaults
were not called *butzle books*,
I was not bitter. And later
when I discovered lovers
did not appreciate being called
poopsie pie, I tried to stop
but every time I went to pinch them
this is what came out.

                    She imagined
all these years that I was Little Debbie
of breakfast food fame. Every letter
she sent contained a picture of me

carved off a donut box, her knife
having rounded precisely,
each fine feature,
each luxurious curl.

Little Debbie,
that consummate image
of sweetness taped to the top
of her letter. Underneath, her words
all running together about thunderstorms
and ministers and tomatoes coming ripe,
words about cataracts fogging her vision,
and missing me. Inside the envelope

folded many times like secret missives
were fashion ads torn from
glamour magazines. In them
models with glossy hair,
rush into city streets
hailing taxis. Always
they are smiling,
always they are raising
their thin arms
in the air.

iii.
I stood vigil over her
when Grandfather died.
She was a wreck
in a cotton nightgown.
Her kingsize bed supported her
wracking side to side like a child
with a high fever. She walked in
while they tried to resuscitate
him. She saw a circle of uniforms,
a nurse forced her from the room,
they lost him anyway,
she never had a chance
to say goodbye. I remember

the day he pulled a rotten molar
from his mouth with a pliers,
the smug look on his face
when he came to the kitchen
to show us the long root.
He said, *I brought this tooth*
with me from Odessa.
                Odessa
Black Sea city of lost
and forgotten memories,
no matter how I stretch
my craft, I still cannot
find your shores. I recall

the long root of a wart
digging deeper into my hand
each day she worried over it.
Wart sounding like *war*

when she told me the word.
For years, I thought I'd had a war
on my hand. Down the street,

she dragged me to the *brauchere,*
an old healer who yodeled,
from her widow's walk
each morning. The *brauchere* tied
a string to my finger, bent over,
crooned to my wormy wound.
Coins were exchanged, the string
was buried outside. Afterward

for my troubles, I got a taste
of Grandpa's rhubarb wine.
The same wine that knocked me
on my ass every time I came over
for Sunday dinner. In those days,

Grandpa made the rounds with his tray
of shot glasses. *One glass*
for everybody, no matter
how small. After dinner
we did tipsy dishes. Grandma
washed, Grandpa dried, I
would put away.

iv.
The last time
I saw Lydia
she was standing
in her kitchen, squat
on her feet like a sugar bowl
in an apron, making sauerkraut—
chopped cabbage heads, ripe
and rank, boiling in kettles
on her stove. *He likes it,*
she said, nodding at Gotthelf,
her stroke-struck second husband.
He was hanging on the ledge
of his chair, smiling
his eye teeth out.

V.
That card game
we used to play, *duruch*,
which I never knew the meaning of
or understood how to play,
but somehow always in the end,
things came around for me. A deuce
took on rare significance,
a red card was considered good.
She would poke me, say the cards
seemed to like me, tell me
I had luck. I always knew
she was lying. Years later

a student of Russian told me *duruch*
means *you fool*. Odessa,
you long cold country,
you were nothing more
than her point of departure.
I was the country
she came to. It's time

to take the wringer washer
out of her basement
and dismantle it, time to untie
the hot towels she wrapped
around my head to relieve
the migraines I inherited
from her. It's time to loosen

their grip. And that old *brauchere*
she took me to who cured me
of ringworm by saying a prayer
and burying a lock
of my hair, it's time
to let her go too. I must

dig up what was buried
and repeat the words
she said. I must
say them to myself.
I must say them
backward.

This
Room
Full of
Nothing

The Weaver

Woman of thread
  woman of silks and yarns
come to the city
  where your dark-hearted sister
    lies in wait
like pest-under-stone
  for a whiff
    for a movement of you

Come to the hair rising
  on the back of the neck
    to the fierce pulsing in arms
Oh weaver woman
  woman of saved string   come
    to the city and see
this vain lump
  I have grown up
    from silence

Come then come
  and we shall unravel
    and weave them well
the many strands of stories
  grown tangled   grown
    convoluted within.

Gravity's First Lesson

tired of raging, i've decided
to go gently. remember that
balloon game we played
as kids, *keep it up, keep*
it up, don't let it touch
the ground. always one kid
willing to grate his cheddar knees
on the carpet. oh, i was good

at that. remember dodge ball.
ten kids in a circle winging
balls at the ones in the middle,
how they always aimed for
the sweet spots—the head
the crotch, the tender budding
breasts. oh, i was the master
dodger. i had a side-step,
a head-fake, a tremendous
high splits jump. oh, no one

could put me out. remember tag,
how we ran with terror from
the one who was it, threw our bodies
down spider-webbed crags,
held our breath behind
heart-pounding corners,
hiding from the one who carried
that terrible transforming touch
on his fingertips. oh, i was never it,
never it, i never wanted

to be it. once, at a rock concert
i saw 50,000 fans moan and heave
to keep a beachball in the air.
50,000 roaring bodies agreeing
with the precision of marines,
on this one thing, *we must*
keep it up, keep it up,
never let it touch
the ground. so,

the earth wants me. is this
gravity's first lesson. tired
of raging, i've decided to
let myself go
gently.

Gatherings

Having let the people of our youth
slip away, we come to these rooms
filled with those from the youths

of others. And you are with the woman
in sequins, and I am with the younger man,
and tonight we ride the conversation

like old sea captains dodging the iceberg
that was our marriage. But I remember
weekday mornings in 1982, your blue Chevy

worn old and silver from the sun, floating
into my alley. You, slamming the screen door
to gather me. Inside, your hands lifted

books from my shelves, hoping only
to trace the words my eyes had seen.
Watching you lift and turn trinkets in the air,

I imagined your touch, so gentle
and full of awe, would always read
my finer lines. Oh, the tricks

some hands can play. Tonight,
I see that touch, soft like a reminder
on her waist, sequins glimmering

in the light, as simply the touch
one stranger reserves
for another, and I know

that when this night is over
we will drift away, caught up
in the streams of others,

drifting and drifting, ceasing
finally to flow to these rooms
where we will find each other.

Losing track eventually
of the comings, of the goings
of the other.

History of a Portrait

Somewhere she has lost her glass
and all that holds her now is a thin frame.
The woman on the wall is veiled in white

that shows its shadows in blue and gray.
Her dress swirls, blown by breezes
from another canvas. A gift from a man

who loved the sight of a face
he could never see, the canvas
still bears traces of a barbeque,

ground into her one mad night
by another man who popped
each egg in the refrigerator

and shredded the houseplants
over the yellow carpet. She is not
dancing. She is shielding herself

from the wind. Scratched, wrinkled
and viewed too many times,
she continues to appear

over the bed, over the couch,
over the kitchen table.
Never once raising her eyes

to see who it is that is going
and who is coming next
in her direction.

Riding Shotgun through
Iowa with Quest

this musician's life.
play until one,
pack up, get paid.
send the dancers
home drunk, sweaty,
clinging to each other.
on the long way home
I ride shotgun with Quest
helping keep watch
over the night. our talk
turns to women and
death, what Quest calls
all things inevitable.
he is not so afraid
of the final embrace
as the moment before,
the arms stretched out
to us, the looking into
the eyes of it. in the dead
of this night, we agree
to trust it, the good faith
of this road running
beneath us. I tell him how
this place is like my home,
where every night
vapor lights burn
in yards, and every morning
farmers rise at dawn to milk
the cows. not for me
that life. in a family
of settlers, I was
the immigrant.
fixing my eye

on the horizon,
setting myself to reel
madly across
this continent. flying
through Iowa, past
cornfields and silos,
the two-storied houses
our dancers have gone
to sleep in, I doze,
wake, doze, to find Quest
hands on the wheel
trying to outdistance
the road. five a.m.
passing a farmyard
I see my father step out
to do the morning chores.
his shadow, bending
to pet the dog becomes
my brother. this is the time
of accidents, the ones
we'll never see.
we pass through
knowing that soon
the sun will show
it's awful face, that soon
even our headlights
will be worthless.

Acts of Preservation

for Thea Kati

i.   Every story she tells
ends with someone dying. From the tip
of her left hand to the tip of her right,
span the yarns of the six generations
she's known. Births. Lives. Deaths.
She pulls them all around, one on top
of the other, until they are knit tightly
together. The easy chair is right where
he left it. On the first night, we are careful
not to sit there, after she says, *No man*
to this earth, will ever take his place.
Out of plastic she brings a scarf he gave her,
the gold silk faded to a soft yellow.
Thirty bucks, she says, this would cost today.

ii.   It has been twenty years
since he left her alone in this cold country
to which he brought her, a seventeen-year-old
bride. It was her sister he was really after,
the most beautiful girl in the village.
The way she tells it, he waited too long
to return home, by the time he got there,
the sister was married. But she reminded him
enough of her sister, so he proposed,
via letter to her father, who replied,
you need to ask my daughter
face-to-face. *Maybe you don't like her.*
Maybe she don't like you. This was 1925.
Erikousa, Greece. She still loves her father
for this.

iii.   And on the last night,
she takes us to her bedroom, throws open
her bureau to the many white shirts cradled
in tissue, some wrapped in the original plastic,
all the price tags say $2.75. Never worn,
she keeps repeating, *never been worn*.
She asks Peter to try one and it fits.
She twirls him around to face the mirror,
runs her old hands down his back.
Such wide shoulders, she says, rolling
the sleeves up to his elbows. And this
is how we spend our last night,
watching Peter try on twenty-five
dress shirts. Even though
they are all white. Even though
she cannot read English, we still know,
they are all the same size.

The Crossing

A little twig in green shuffled her tennies
the corner of 10th and 12th this morning.

Impatient for fluorescent orange crossing guards,
she shifted side to side stomping her feet.

There was a general rush of traffic, workers,
late for work, trying to wrench distance

from each second. I had a left on green.
It was my turn. Cars collected behind me.

She started off the curb, then jumped back,
her face cast down to the concrete,

all her safety lessons unlearned.
I signaled her safe and she bolted,

little legs like tiny gears motoring
the distance of a crossing.

She made small progress
through car grilles and paint striping.

Mounting the curb on the other side,
she ambled down the sidewalk,

her body swinging loosely to school.
I would have turned immediately,

to recover the distance I had lost,
but I noticed, idling in the lane

next to me, a couple with glasses,
mid-fifties, stopped on the green,

both heads turned far
down the sidewalk. The man

kept his hands on the wheel.
The woman looked like

she was about to say something.

Small Town Cafe

Tonight while the men
have gone home to their wives
and the teenagers to their cars,
only the three old bachelors
full of coffee and gossip,
sit by the window and watch
as traffic rolls by. The cook

in greasy glasses, has emerged
from the cave of the kitchen,
with a yellow fly swatter
in her hand, bent to kill
all winged intruders.
I follow in white shoes
wiping the splattered tables
with this wet rag. The owner

smokes and watches from behind
the counter. She has designer
eyeglasses and fingernails
and a limp that even her mink
won't let you forget. Coffee
is ten cents, but if a strange car
pulls up, full of new suits
with briefcases, she will lift
herself from the stool, limp
across the room and whisper,
charge them twenty-five.

Grandfather's Hands

Grandfather's hands in the sausage tub,
where I sat for hours and watched him

add salt, pepper, garlic, salt, pepper,
garlic, then knead everything together

with his hairy knuckles. His hairy knuckles
reminding me of Brezhnev's eyebrows

on the steering wheel, driving me
to school in the fan-tailed Chevy

at five miles an hour. Left turns
taking an eternity of stutter steps

inch-by-inch, not hand-over-hand
like my brother was learning

in Driver's Ed. Grandfather's hands
on the wheel, Memorial Day drives

to Tappen, to put flowers
on the boys' graves. The three

small wreaths riding with me
in the back seat like well-behaved

children. The silence in the car
afterward, except for the sound

of the blinker from the last left turn,
clicking on and off all the way home.

Riding Back to Town

Just as he came from water,
so he returned to it.
His preoccupation,
the final years, was fishing.
Every day he'd load
his tackle box and drive
thirty miles to the nearest lake,
coming home at sundown
with nothing, as far as I
ever saw. I went with him once.
Riding home in silence
I felt good. In the presence
of his siren sisters-in-law,
he could sit for hours, hands
folded over his stomach.
To all questions he gave
answers without handles.
We wandered off, replies
clutched under arms
like immigrants with poor
luggage. He is gone,
a long time now. Strange
how this thirty miles
reminds me of him.
In the distance
a stream of water
moves across
a field of stones.
I get the feeling
I'm riding back to town
with no fish.

Resurrection

A rose by your bedside you would never know,
the nurses tried to tell me. I tried to tell them

how you always knew to plant the tulips
inside the dahlias, inside the gladioli

and leave a space in the middle,
the place I always found you

when I came to visit. Hard to believe,
you gone, almost two years now

and this lily, given to me
last Easter to help me through

the first year, how I swore
I'd keep it alive all year.

You would have laughed at my despair
when it began to make its slow descent

back to the earth. First the white trumpets
dropping off, then leaf after leaf retracting

until all that was left was the brown stalk
which I cut down to nothing. It disgusted

me so. *Alone, through a valley, we all
must walk*, an old man told me

at your funeral. You would have laughed
at my surprise when the green shoots

appeared. *Weeds*, I thought
but watered them, and now they are lilies

three of them, climbing back out
of themselves, preparing to tell it

all over again. These things we call miracles.
It would be enough to make you laugh.

The Blizzard Rope

I have not forgotten,
ten and still holding
the blizzard rope you tied
around my waist, winter
of sixty-six. You said,
you are home base,
and stepped out
into weather. Snow

like a house built
around us. Holsteins
holding their milk
in the hungry barn.
You had no choice.
The straight path
you walked every day
a mystery, in this weather.
I have not forgotten,
thirty-three and holding
the blizzard rope.

White-out, you step out.
Your fine hands
climbing weather,
your dark coat, lost
to the great white.
Your footsteps
filling now with
weather. The line
has grown icy.
The weather worsens.
I am home base.
Go where you will.

Somewhere in a House
Where You are Not

There is sunlight coming through windows
somewhere in a house where you are not.

An old man and old woman eating breakfast
to the sound of the clock, out of words,

empty of thoughts, but for who died this year
and of what. If you follow the sun to that house

you will find the long lost driveway
that no highway intersects, the loose gravel

crackling under your wheels, the sun breaking
cleanly free of a horizon. You must park.

You must come to an absolute halt
outside the house where you are not,

letting your many necessary miles drop
from your bones like dust. Sit and wait.

Do not fear the mop-faced dog. He pounds
his tail for you. He is uninterested

in your tires. The old woman will soon come,
peeking through the ancient blinds, saying,

who on earth, and seeing your face
will hold out her hands, warm and soft

as good black dirt, and take you inside,
the house filling with your arrival,

the old man smiling his surprised skeleton smile,
the old woman asking, have you come far,

was it a long drive, are you hungry, are you
tired, to which you may answer, yes

and lie down in the bed they have kept
empty in your absence, reserved for the day

you would need this room full of nothing,
but rare morning light, and the stroke

of an old brown hand, inviting you
to rest, to sleep, to feel the earth

revolve slowly around and around
without you.

About the author

Debra Marquart, a native of Napoleon, North Dakota, has a Master's Degree in Liberal Arts from Moorhead State University, and an M.A. in English from Iowa State University. She currently teaches creative writing at Drake University.

During the 1970s and 1980s, Ms. Marquart was a rock and roll musician, traveling on the road through the U.S. and Canada for seven years. At present she is a collaborating member of "The Bone People," a musical/performance art project in which she attempts to fuse her poetry with elements of jazz and rhythm and blues.

Debra Marquart's poetry and prose have appeared in *New Letters, River City, North Dakota Quarterly,* and other magazines. Her poem "Somewhere in a House Where You are Not" was recently chosen by Charles Simic as the winner of the Guy Owen Poetry Prize.

About the cover artist

The cover of *Everything's a Verb* features "Surfacing," a painting by Peter Dean. Born in Berlin in 1934, Mr. Dean came to the United States in 1938, where he lived in New York City. After attending Cornell University for two years, Mr. Dean transferred to the University of Wisconsin where he graduated in 1958. Peter Dean died in March, 1993, after a battle with Lou Gehrig's disease. He is survived by his wife Lori, and son Gregory.